MEMORABLE
STORIES
WITH A MESSAGE

MEMORABLE STORIES

WITH A MESSAGE

BOYD K. PACKER

WITH ARTWORK BY THE AUTHOR

DESERET BOOK
SALT LAKE CITY, UTAH

Cover art by Boyd K. Packer

Library of Congress Catalog Card Number 00-130363

ISBN 1-57345-788-4

Printed in the United States of America   72082-6653

10   9   8   7   6   5   4   3

CONTENTS

1

BEAR WITNESS AND BE AT PEACE

Some years ago, at a time when a Church member's campaign for national office was creating much interest, I was invited to speak to a group at Harvard University. Both faculty members and students were to be present. I, of course, hoped that the gospel message would be accepted and that the meeting would end in a harmony of views. As I prayed that this might result, there came to me the strong impression that this petition would not be granted. I determined that, however preposterous talk about angels and golden plates and restoration might be to my audience, I would teach the truth with quiet confidence, for I have a testimony of the truth. If some must come from the meeting unsettled and disturbed, it would not be *me*. Let *them* be disturbed, if they would.

It was as the Spirit foretold. Some in the group shook their heads in amazement, even cynical amusement, that anyone could believe such things. But I was at peace, I had taught the truth, and they could accept it or reject it, as they pleased.

There is always the hope, and often it is true, that in a group one person with an open mind may admit one simple thought: "Could it possibly be true?" Combine that thought with sincere prayer and one more soul enters a private sacred grove to find the answer to the question, "Which of all the churches is true, and which should I join?"

As I grow in age and experience, I grow ever *less* concerned over whether others agree with us. I grow ever *more* concerned that they understand us. If they do understand, they have their agency and can accept or reject the gospel as they please.

It is not an easy thing for us to defend the position that bothers so many others. But never be ashamed of the gospel of Jesus Christ. Never apologize for the sacred doctrines of the gospel. Never feel inadequate and unsettled because you cannot explain them to the satisfaction of all who might inquire of you. Do not be ill at ease or uncomfortable because you can give little more than your conviction.

Be assured that, if you will explain what you know and testify of what you feel, you may plant a seed that will one day grow and blossom into a testimony of the gospel of Jesus Christ.

I bear testimony that The Church of Jesus Christ of Latter-day Saints is, as the Lord declared, the only true and living church upon the face of the earth; that with it He is well pleased, speaking of the Church collectively; and that if individually we are humble and faithful we can stand approved of Him.

If we can stand without shame, without hesitancy, without embarrassment, without reservation, to bear witness that the gospel has been restored, that there are prophets and Apostles upon the earth, that the truth is available for all mankind—if we can do this the Lord's Spirit will be with us. And that assurance can be affirmed to others.

The voice of the Spirit speaks gently, prompting you what to do or what to say, or it may caution or warn you. Ignore or disobey these promptings, and the Spirit will leave you. It is your choice—your agency.
(From "Personal Revelation: The Gift, the Test, and the Promise," ENSIGN, November 1990, p. 60)

2

CAN YOU ANSWER YES?

A friend of mine once told me of an experience at a university when, as a young Ph.D., he was being interviewed for a position. The dean asked if he was a Mormon, and he said he was. The next question was, "Are you a good member of your church?" He said, "Well, I try to be," or something to that effect. The dean got a bit irritated—he really wanted to know. "Are you or are you not a good member of your church?" His reply was "Yes sir!" He told me that there were few things more important or precious to him than when he had to stand up and say, "Yes sir, I am a good member of the Church."

Each of us should ask himself or herself that question. Can you answer yes? Or do you stutter, ". . . A good member in all but . . ." Are you?

3

DON'T FORGET THEM

I have come to know firsthand that a very powerful and abiding spirit broods over the work of searching through the records for the names and life stories of our kindred dead. For several years a major portion of my prayers and efforts was devoted to the temple and genealogical work of the Church.

There is something about it that we can feel but that we cannot explain—a very moving spirit, urging us ahead, as though some were pleading with us not to lose them and not to forget them.

A few years ago a mother told me her life story. She had been abandoned by her husband and left to raise a little boy. When he was nine years old he contracted a fatal disease. He came to know somehow, in his little boy mind, that he would not live. And for the last two or three weeks of his life he would cling to his mother and say, "Mama, you won't forget me, will you? Mama, please don't forget me. Mama, I won't be forgotten, will I?"

I was deeply moved, for I sensed that in the pleading of this little boy something of the feelings of every one of us is exposed, hoping that somehow we will at least be remembered, hoping that there will be something about us worth remembering. Our forebears surely felt that too.

4

A HOST OF GOALS

Donna and I attended an unusual holiday dinner at the home of one of our beloved friends. It was a New Year's Eve party. Our host had an activity for the evening. He read a quotation from Heber C. Kimball: "I have said often, you may write blessings for yourselves, and insert every good thing you can think of, and it will all come to pass on your heads, if you do right" (from an address given in the Old Tabernacle, August 1853).

He gave each of us a sheet of paper and an envelope and suggested we write upon the paper the things we hoped to achieve in the new year. We were asked to seal the envelope and put our name on it.

"I will take these to the bank and put them in the vault," he said. "A year from now we will meet again and have a dinner and I will deliver them to you. And we will tell, if we wish, how nearly we have achieved our goals."

We thoughtfully set our goals that night and sealed them up, and they were delivered to the vault to lay unopened for a full year.

Six things were on our list, each relating to a blessing for someone dear. Each seemed near to the impossible. One, for instance, related to a sister and temple marriage. Worthiness was no problem; it was her body—so crippled with disease that a temple session was out of the question—or was it?

The year rolled by and the envelopes were delivered to us again.

During the year, with those goals in mind we had prayed now and then, and then little opportunities or advantages came by. They would have gone unnoticed if we had not set the goals.

We were able to move forward, first with one goal, then with another. Five impossible things had happened. The sixth related to the solution of a problem of a friend.

It was on New Year's Eve that I received a telephone call from across the country. My friend excitedly told me that his problem had been solved. He knew nothing of the notes in the envelope.

5

FIRST THE RULE

On one occasion when I was president of the New England Mission we were holding a Relief Society conference of several hundred women. Our Relief Society president was a convert. We were trying to get our sewing circles and gossip festivals turned into Relief Societies. We were setting the standards for Relief Society, and this lovely little sister was told to teach the sisters what a Relief Society should be.

A woman stood up in the audience and defied her. She said: "You don't understand. Things are different up in Vermont. This is different, we are an exception. We can't do that. You must make an exception."

The Relief Society president was quite puzzled at this confrontation. She turned around and looked at me, pleading for help. I thought she was doing pretty well, so I motioned for her to proceed. She did, and what she said next was so profound that I told her after the meeting I would be quoting that across the world, since I was sure it came by inspiration.

She stood there frightened and puzzled for a few minutes.

That defiant woman, who was something of a ringleader representing a faction, kept talking for a minute, reemphasizing that they were an exception.

Then Sister Baker quietly but firmly said: "Dear sister, we'd like not to take care of the exception first. We'll see to the rule first and then we'll take care of the exception."

Now, what are you to do in your lives? Accommodate the rule first! If you're to be an exception or if others are to be an exception, that will become obvious in the inspiration that comes. But there is great power and great safety in holding to the scriptures and having an abounding obedience to our constituted priesthood authority. We are able to pray and receive revelation on our own, then to obediently say, "Lord, I don't ask to be an exception."

6

MOTHER IN THE HOME

I was seated in the kitchen some time ago when my wife came from the living room. She had a puzzled expression on her face, and she turned and walked back into the other room. Sensing that something was wrong, I followed.

It turned out she had come through the room and noticed our son sitting on the couch, his arms folded, looking out on a beautiful sunlit day. Had I come through the room I would have thought, "Thank goodness, he is quiet for once," because I am a dad, and I just have a head. But she is a mom and she has a heart, and very often the heart will know things that the head will scarcely understand.

I watched with reverence as she sat beside him, put her arm round his shoulder, and said, "Son, anything wrong?"

"No."

"Everything all right?"

"Yes."

With each question she pulled him just a little tighter, and he is as tall as she is. Finally, she said, "Did anything happen at school today?" Then his eyes started to swim and his lip started to quiver, and he sobbed out his tale of how the world had all fallen apart that day.

I watched with love and reverence as she explained to him in a few words how he could apologize the next day and get the world back on its axis. And the genius of it all was that he did not even know he would be making an apology. It was because she was there in the home, because she was present as a parent, and because she was able to see and to feel and to know.

On another occasion, our second grader was offering the family prayer. At the close of his prayer he said, "And Heavenie Father, please bless us that we will be good in school and not get sent to the principal's office and get a talking to." That day Sister Packer found time to go to the school. You see, there had been a little trouble born, in the first instance, outside the home. The older son brought it home with him, and with the love that only a mother possesses, she had reached in and located it and destroyed it. This second little trouble was not quite so easy. It took a dad and a mom and a principal and a teacher and a little boy and some prayer, but that trouble also was eventually eradicated because there was a mother in the home.

7

THAT DAY WE DID SEE

In a testimony meeting, a friend of mine told of a conversation he'd had that week with a fellow employee in a business establishment. My friend had regarded him as an active member, a faithful member of the Church always, and yet in this conversation his coworker made the comment that he didn't believe there was much inspiration in the way people were called to office in the Church. He said they were called from desperation or something else but there couldn't be much inspiration in it.

I don't know whether that comment was sparked by a call the coworker had received himself for which he felt unworthy; or perhaps he had been offended by someone who was called and who was, he thought, ineligible; or maybe he referred to one of the few—and there are few—who accept a call in the Church unwillingly and really fail to perform. For the one who doubts the influence of inspiration in Church calls to office and for us all, I quote a verse from the Doctrine and Covenants. The Lord is speaking: "I command and men obey not; I revoke and they receive not the blessing. Then they say in their hearts: This is not the work of the Lord, for his promises are not fulfilled. But wo unto such, for their reward lurketh beneath, and not from above" (D&C 58:32–33).

Let us consider the quiet miracle relating to the calling of members of the Church to office and their response to that call. That's a miracle by which I never fail to be humbled— that process by which a person is designated to receive a call in the Church and the witness he receives as he answers it. The suggestion that there is no inspiration in it is something we have to contemplate.

Early in my Church leadership experience I learned a very important lesson. I think it was the second time I had met Elder Harold B. Lee; I had been introduced to him once before.

I was serving as a member of a stake high council, and on one occasion the stake president presented in our meeting the name of a certain man to be called to a position of leadership in the stake. I was teaching seminary at the time, and Brother Leon Strong, also a seminary teacher, had talked to me a time or two about this man. We had commented on what an able man he was and how sad it was that he couldn't do more than he did in Church service because of a handicap of his wife's. She had one personality trait that I think could be characterized by the term *malicious*.

When the stake president presented the name of this man for a presiding office in the stake and called for a vote, Brother Strong and I cast negative votes. That is rather unusual. The president talked it over for a few minutes and then said that he felt he'd like to proceed anyway, and asked if we would sustain him in issuing this call. Immediately the issue changed. In my mind, then, it was a vote to sustain the stake president, not necessarily a vote for placing this man in the office; and when the president called for a vote, Brother Strong and I joined the other ten members of the stake high council in voting affirmatively.

When our stake conference was held a month or two later, when the ordinations were to take place, Elder Harold B. Lee of the Council of the Twelve was the visitor. After the conference we assembled in the stake center for the ordinations. Elder Lee ordained and set apart a bishop and his counselors and some others, and then this man was called forth to be ordained by the member of the Council of the Twelve. Brother Strong nudged me—we were sitting together—and with a smile on his face he leaned over and said, "Well, Brother Packer, now we'll see whether this Church is run by revelation."

Elder Lee put his hands on the man's head, began the usual introductory words to an ordination, then hesitated. Then he said words to this effect: "The other blessings relating to your activities and life and occupation that you've heard pronounced upon the others here apply to you as well, but there is a special blessing." And then that man received the longest blessing, the most pointed of them all; and in reality it was not a blessing for him but a blessing for his wife. It was a very interesting thing to observe.

When the meeting was over, immediately I went to Brother Lee and said, "Did you know this brother before you ordained him?"

"No," he said. "I didn't know him. I think I hadn't seen him till I came into this room."

I said, "He received a very unusual blessing."

And Elder Lee said, "Yes, I felt that."

Later, the president of the stake explained: "I meant to

talk to Elder Lee about that and tell him that here was a man who had need of a special blessing, but in the press of business we just didn't have time."

And so Brother Strong was right. That day we did see whether this Church is run by revelation.

*P*ersonal testimony is confirmed to us initially and is reaffirmed and enlarged thereafter through a harmonious combining of both the intellect and the spirit.
(From "Reverence Invites Revelation," ENSIGN, November 1991, p. 21)

8

HELPING CHILDREN APPRECIATE THE HOME TEACHERS

One young elder is not really strong spiritually. He's trying to get a small business established and it takes more time than he has. He feels that he must accommodate the world a bit. After all, these men of the world seem to be the key to his financial success.

He's on the list of those about whom his quorum president and his bishop have serious concern. He did accept the assignment to go home teaching—primarily because his wife was urging him to. (Again we see the good influence of a righteous woman.)

His companion is a young teacher. At that age he's innocent of any real desire to go home teaching.

Your children are gathered around the television set watching a show. The hero is fleeing from enemies and is swept from the saddle by the limb of a tree and rolls over the edge of a cliff. He hangs there by his fingers. He glances over his shoulder and below is a writhing pit of rattlesnakes. It is in this position that the enemies find him and gleefully begin to stomp on his fingers.

And then, just at that moment, the doorbell rings!

"Children, turn off the television set, the home teachers are here." At this command the children who are too old to complain twist their faces in disapproval. The home teachers get "that look."

In the middle of an all-too-brief discussion, the youngest one of course will say, "Mama, when are they going to leave?"

And leave they do, after briefly commenting on the weather and dryly mentioning that anyone can see that everyone in the family is all right and that they have several other places they should visit that night.

When the door closes behind them, your children rush back to the television set. When all's said and done, it was hardly worth interrupting the television show for what they accomplished.

What do we do about that? There are some small and little things that bring great things to pass. You, dear sisters, can with very little effort transform it if you will.

The mother can keep a welcome waiting for the priesthood home teachers when they call.

For instance, we know enough when our children are playing outside with all the neighbors, not to summarily announce, "It's time to come in." That would make the storm clouds gather. "Can't we play just one more game? Do we have to come in now? We just got started. Some of the kids just got here."

You've heard all of that.

How much wiser it is to announce, "In fifteen minutes it will be time to come in." By that time the game is over and the children respond.

I know enough not to march through the house demanding that the children immediately go to bed.

Our daughter will just be hemming a skirt she has made. The other two, who have worked hard on their lessons, are now finding a few minutes before bedtime to play with their dolls.

One son is at work at the workbench making a model stagecoach, and another is getting his gym clothes ready for school. Our eight-year-old is working at one of over a hundred hobbies to which he is devoted.

An abrupt announcement and the clouds gather again.

How much better to give notice: "Children, in fifteen minutes it will be time to go to bed."

Of course, we could have agreed in a family home evening long since what the hour of bedtime was, but a gentle reminder fifteen minutes before and the skirt is finished, the dolls are put away, the other things are set aside.

Whatever it was our eight-year-old was doing is scattered on the floor, waiting for some assignment to pick them up—a ceremony that is part of the life of a healthy, normal eight-year-old.

I can imagine that any mother could give encouragement in the family home evening to the idea that we would welcome the home teachers.

They should, of course, make appointments first. But suppose they did arrive in the middle of a favorite television program.

The children might well have been told long since that if there is some interruption when the home teachers come there will be extra privileges for good deportment.

Make it so that home teaching is associated with pleasant

things in the minds of your little ones, and in the minds of your home teachers.

9

FOLLOW THE BEAM

It has been many years, but I have not forgotten that as pilots in World War II we did not have the electronic equipment that we have today. Our hope in a storm was to follow a radio beam.

A steady signal, and you were on course. If you moved to one side of the steady signal, it would break up to a "dit-da," the Morse code for the letter A.

If you strayed to the other side of the signal, the beam would break up into a "da-dit," the morse code signal for N.

In stormy weather there was always static and interference. But the life of many a pilot has depended on his hearing, above the roar of the engines and through all the static and interference, that sometimes weak signal from a distant airfield.

There is a spiritual beam with a constant signal. If you know how to pray and how to listen, spiritually listen, you may move through life—through clear weather, through storms, through wars, through peace—and be all right.

10

KNOWLEDGE IS NOT AN END

I was acquainted with a Harvard professor of economics. He once told me that when he was a student in Germany someone asked him what he intended to do with the knowledge he was gaining. He said the question made him very angry. Why did he have to do anything with it? Was knowledge not worth acquiring for itself alone?

Somewhere in the economic difficulties we now suffer are the theories of the professor of economics who thought knowledge was an end in itself.

Years ago there was a student at Columbia University who was known as the "perennial student." He had been left an inheritance which stipulated that it should continue as long as he was engaged in collegiate study. Thereafter, the income was to go to a charity.

This man remained a student until he died. It was said that he had been granted every degree offered by Columbia University and had taken practically every course. No field of knowledge was foreign to him. He was probably more widely read than the best of his professors. He was described as the "epitome of erudition." But he could not possibly be described as educated. He fit the description of those spoken of in the scripture who are "ever learning, and never able to come to the knowledge of the truth" (2 Timothy 3:7). He was inherently selfish. What a pity! What a waste!

There are complementary and tempering teachings in the scriptures which bring a balanced knowledge of truth.
(From "The Pattern of Our Parentage,"
ENSIGN, November 1984, p. 66)

11

NEVER RIDICULE THE UNFORTUNATE

I must say this to parents. It is not unusual for foolish children and some very thoughtless adults to make light of those with disabilities. The mimicking or teasing or ridiculing of those with handicaps is cruel. Such an assault can inflict deeper pain than can physical punishment—more painful because it is undeserved. It is my conviction that such brutality will not, in the eternal scheme of things, go unanswered, and there will come a day of recompense.

My mother taught us when we were very young that we must never ridicule the unfortunate. Her mother died when she was six. My mother worked in the fields from a very early age. One day some teenagers were picking fruit. One of the girls laughingly mimicked one who suffered from cerebral palsy, saying, "Look who I am," and she named the handicapped person. They all laughed as she threw herself into a stumbling walk. Suddenly she fell as if struck down. They gathered around her in great fright. Presently she recovered, but there was no more fun at the expense of those with disabilities. Mother never forgot what she saw, nor to teach a lesson from it.

Parents, take time in the next home evening to caution your family never to amuse themselves at the expense of those with disabilities or of any whose face or form or personality does not fit the supposed ideal or whose skin is too light or too dark to suit their fancy. Teach them that they, in their own way, should become like angels who "move the water" (see John 5:2–4), healing a spirit by erasing loneliness, embarrassment, or rejection.

The study of the doctrines of the gospel will improve behavior quicker than a study of behavior will improve behavior. (From "Little Children," ENSIGN, November 1986, p. 17)

12

THE CURSE OF PROFANITY

Years ago I went with one of my brothers to tow in a wrecked car. It was a single-car accident, and the car was demolished; the driver, though unhurt, had been taken to the hospital for treatment of shock and for examination.

The next morning he came asking for his car, anxious to be on his way. When he was shown the wreckage, his pent-up emotions and disappointment, sharpened perhaps by his misfortune, exploded in a long stream of profanity. So obscene and biting were his words that they exposed years of practice with profanity. His words were heard by other customers, among them women, and must have touched their ears like acid.

One of my brothers crawled from beneath the car, where he had been working with a large wrench. He too was upset, and with threatening gestures of the wrench (mechanics will know that a 16-inch crescent wrench is a formidable weapon) he ordered the man off the premises. "We don't have to listen to that kind of language here," he said. And the customer left, cursing more obscenely than before.

Much later in the day he reappeared, subdued, penitent; and avoiding everyone else he found my brother.

"I have been in the hotel room all day," he said, "lying on the bed tormented. I can't tell you how utterly ashamed I am for what happened this morning. My conduct was inexcusable. I have been trying to think of some justification, and I can think of only one thing. In all my life, never, not once, have I been told that my language was not acceptable. I have always talked that way. You were the first one who ever told me that my language was out of order."

Isn't it interesting that a man could grow to maturity, the victim of such a vile habit, and never meet a protest? How tolerant we have become, and how quickly we are moving! A generation ago writers of newspapers, editors of magazines, and particularly the producers of motion pictures carefully censored profane and obscene words.

All that has now changed. It began with the novel. Writers, insisting that they must portray life as it is, began to put into the mouths of their characters filthy, irreverent expressions. These words on the pages of books came before the eyes of all ages and imprinted themselves on the minds of our youth.

Carefully (we are always led carefully), profanity has inched and nudged and pushed its way relentlessly into the motion picture and the magazine, and now even newspapers print verbatim comments, the likes of which would have been considered intolerable a generation ago.

13

THE TRUST OF LITTLE CHILDREN

Some years ago, Dr. Faun Hunsaker, then president of the Southern States Mission, was invited to stay at the home of a member. They arrived after the children were in bed.

He occupied the parents' bedroom, and during the night heard the door open and the sound of little feet. A little boy frightened by a bad dream had come to his parents' bed for comfort.

Sensing that something was different, the little boy felt Brother Hunsaker's face. So he spoke quietly to the child. The startled youngster said, "You're not my daddy!"

"No, I'm not your daddy."

"Did my daddy say you could sleep here?"

"Yes, your daddy said I could sleep here."

With that the little youngster crawled into bed with Brother Hunsaker and was soon asleep.

There is much in the scriptures about little children.

The Psalmist wrote, "Children are an heritage of the Lord" (Psalm 127:3).

The Savior gave the ever-familiar plea, "Suffer the little

children to come unto me, and forbid them not: for of such is the kingdom of heaven" (Mark 10:14).

When His disciples asked, "Who is the greatest in the kingdom of heaven? . . . Jesus called a little child unto him, and set him in the midst of them, and said, . . . Whosoever . . . shall humble himself as this little child, the same is greatest in the kingdom of heaven. And whoso shall receive one such little child in my name receiveth me" (Matthew 18:1–5).

*E*ach time a child is born, the world is renewed in innocence. *(From "Little Children," ENSIGN, November 1986, p. 17)*

14

THE ORDER OF THINGS

Principle: A prime attribute of a good leader is to be a good follower. In a meeting with bishops, a new and struggling bishop once asked me, "How do I get people to follow me? I have called nine sisters to be president of the Primary and none has accepted." There was a good humor and pleasant spirit in the meeting which made it an ideal teaching moment. I answered that I doubted that he had "called" any of the nine sisters. He must only have asked or invited them.

I told him that if he had earnestly prayed and counseled with his counselors as to who should preside over the Primary, the first sister would have accepted the call. Perhaps he might have discovered in the interview some reason why it was not advisable or timely for that sister to serve and excused her from serving. But surely not more than one or two. If that many sisters turned down the call, something was out of order—the unwritten order.

15

WASHED CLEAN

During World War II, I had an experience. Our bomber crew had been trained at Langley Field, Virginia, to use the latest invention—radar. We were ordered to the West Coast and then on to the Pacific.

We were transported on a freight train with boxcars fitted with narrow bedsprings that could be pulled down from the wall at night. There were no dining cars. Instead, camp kitchens were set up in boxcars with dirt floors.

We were dressed in light-colored summer uniforms. The baggage car got sidetracked, so we had no change of clothing during the six-day trip. It was very hot crossing Texas and Arizona. Smoke and cinders from the engine made it very uncomfortable. There was no way to bathe or to wash our uniforms. We rolled into Los Angeles one morning—a grubby-looking outfit—and were told to return to the train that evening.

We thought first of food. The ten of us in our crew pooled our money and headed for the best restaurant we could find.

It was crowded, so we joined a long line waiting to be seated. I was first, just behind some well-dressed women. Even without turning around, the stately woman in front of me soon became aware that we were there.

She turned and looked at us. Then she turned and looked me over from head to toe. There I stood in that sweaty, dirty, sooty, wrinkled uniform. She said in a tone of disgust, "My, what untidy men!" All eyes turned to us.

No doubt she wished we were not there; I shared her wish. I felt as dirty as I was, uncomfortable, and ashamed.

Later, when I began a serious study of the scriptures, I noticed references to being spiritually clean. One verse says, "Ye would be more miserable to dwell with a holy and just God, under a consciousness of your filthiness before him, than ye would to dwell with the damned souls in hell" (Mormon 9:4).

16

To the Edge of the Light

Shortly after I was called as a General Authority, I went to Elder Harold B. Lee for counsel. He listened very carefully to my problem and suggested that I see President David O. McKay. President McKay counseled me as to the direction I should go. I was very willing to be obedient but saw no possible way for me to do as he counseled me to do.

I returned to Elder Lee and told him that I saw no way to move in the direction I was counseled to go. He said, "The trouble with you is you want to see the end from the beginning." I replied that I would like to see at least a step or two ahead. Then came the lesson of a lifetime: "You must learn to walk to the edge of the light, and then a few steps into the darkness, then the light will appear and show the way before you." Then he quoted these eighteen words from the Book of Mormon: "Dispute not because ye see not, for ye receive no witness until after the trial of your faith" (Ether 12:6).

17

GIVE VISION AND ENCOURAGEMENT

Some years ago I was near our front gate splitting rails for a fence. A young man came to make a delivery. He had recently returned from overseas combat duty. He had falsified his age and left school to join the Marines. When I asked about his future plans, he didn't know. Jobs were scarce; he had no skills to offer.

I counseled him to go back to high school and get his diploma. He thought he couldn't do that; he was too old now. "If you do it," I told him, "you probably will not exactly fit in. And the students will call you the 'old man' or 'grandpa.' But you faced an enemy in combat; surely you've got the courage to face that."

The lesson is this: I only spent ten minutes with him, sitting on a log by our front gate. I did not build a school or ask the Church to build one. I did not pay his tuition or prepare his lessons. What he needed was some direction, some counsel, some encouragement, and some vision. In this case he took the counsel and returned to school. Now he has a family and an occupation.

I only gave him the vision and encouragement. It does not take additional Church budget to do that. That is the responsible role of every priesthood leader in counseling members on careers. We must help people to help themselves.

18

ONE CONFERENCE ATTENDER

The General Conferences of the Latter-day Saints are one of the great outstanding testimonies . . . of the divinity of the work in which we are engaged" (Heber J. Grant, in Conference Report, October 1933, p. 118).

What of those who attend conference? Perhaps we could introduce just one of them. Some time ago there came to a conference the religion editor of a large newspaper. He came across the country to get the "feel" of the conference.

Before the opening of a session, we came down the aisle of the building. It was filled to capacity. He noticed a middle-aged man, dressed unpretentiously, sitting next to the aisle, and asked to be introduced. We found him to be from the West Coast, a convert to the Church. As I recall, he had once been a member of the same church to which the editor belonged. He was a counselor in a bishopric. The interview proceeded something like this:

"How long have you been a member of the Church?"

"About eight years."

"Did you join the first time the missionaries contacted you?"

"Oh, no. It took me several weeks before I joined the Church." Then he added with a smile, "I don't like to rush into things."

"They tell me," the reporter inquired, "that the President of your church is a prophet. Is that true?"

"Oh yes! I know him to be a prophet of God, just as much a prophet as any of the biblical prophets."

"Are you paid for your service in the Church?"

"Oh yes!" he said. "Generously paid—in blessings, not money. It seems that the principle of tithing requires that we pay for the privilege."

The editor, satisfied with the interview, turned to leave. Then, as an afterthought, he turned again with another question and said, "Tell me, why—why do you pay tithing?"

I noticed that the good brother's countenance became very serious, and there was a brimming bit of emotion in his eyes as he softly answered in a single word: "Obedience."

19

FOLLOW THAT SPIRIT

One of our sons served a mission in Australia. They were assigned to a small town, about three thousand people. They lived with a member of the Church. She was a widow, an older woman. She treated the missionaries very kindly.

One day my son and his companion were out tracting. They were knocking on doors clear across the town. My son felt something. He turned to his companion and said, "I think we should go home now."

"But we are just getting started," his companion answered. Without waiting, my son turned and headed back for home. He did not walk, he ran. He's a very tall boy and can run very fast. His companion could hardly keep up with him.

As they came through the gate of that little house, they found this little lady lying amid the flowers in the garden. She had gone out early to work in the garden. As she began to work, she felt some heavy pains. She tried to go to the house, but she couldn't walk. So she prayed, "Oh Lord, help me! Please send help!" And then she collapsed into the flowers.

My son didn't hear anything. No one told him anything. He felt like they should go home. He was a missionary. Missionaries learn to follow that spirit.

*T*he patterns of revelation are not dramatic. The voice of inspiration is a still voice, a small voice. There need be no trance, no sanctimonious declaration. It is quieter and simpler than that. (From "Revelation in a Changing World," ENSIGN, November 1989, p. 14)

20

CONSTITUTED AUTHORITY

The forty-second section of the Doctrine and Covenants contains this verse: "Again, I say unto you, that it shall not be given to any one to go forth to preach my gospel, or to build up my church, except he be ordained by some one who has authority, and it is known to the church that he has authority and has been regularly ordained by the heads of the church" (D&C 42:11).

In our day it would be difficult for someone to get off a plane somewhere and represent himself, for instance, as a member of the Council of the Twelve and proceed to give instruction or to perform ordinations that would be counterfeit. This couldn't be done without being detected. We're too well known in a very interesting way.

That brings to mind an experience when my oldest son took his little family to tithing settlement. When they went to the bishop's office there was a picture of all of the General Authorities. Our tiny granddaughter noticed the picture and got all excited, saying, "Oh, Grandpa, Grandpa!" My daughter-in-law lifted her up and she pointed to Brother McConkie!

Some time ago my wife and I were coming home from New Zealand. We had left Auckland about midnight and landed in Papeete, Tahiti, to change planes in the wee hours of the morning. We had an hour or two to spend and were waiting for our flight to come in. A Pan American plane landed and we were watching that plane taxi in. I didn't know where it was from or where it was going, but I said to my wife, "I will know someone on that flight." It was just a flight out in the Pacific in the wee hours of a Monday morning.

I went out and stood by the gate. I knew one man as he got off. Four other people came up and said, "You're Brother Packer, aren't you?" That's a handicap sometimes to us personally, but there's a great protection in that for the Church.

Once I was with President Kimball in New York. We had gone to tape an interview that was going to go on the CBS nationwide broadcast. It was a beautiful Saturday morning in April and we decided to walk up Fifth Avenue to the mission home. Thousands of people were out walking and President Kimball said, "Look at all of these people—and they're all ours. They all should have the gospel and not a one of them knows us. All of them are strangers to us," he said.

"I know how we can find someone we know," I said.

"How can we find them?" he asked.

We were passing a little French restaurant with tables sitting out on the sidewalk. I said, in a joking way, "We can just step over there and order coffee, and someone will find us in a hurry!"

Just as I said that I heard the words, "Brother Kimball!

Brother Kimball!" Out of the crowd came the wife of a stake president!

The point I make is that this phrase from Timothy strikes me as being monumentally important: "But continue thou in the things which thou hast learned and hast been assured of, knowing of whom thou hast learned them" (2 Timothy 3:14). In the pattern of constituted authority in the Church we always know where revelation comes from.

There is purpose in members of the Church everywhere in the world being able to identify the general and local authorities. In that way they can know of whom they learn.
(From "From Such Turn Away," ENSIGN, *May 1985, p. 34)*

21

COURTSHIP AND COUNSEL

I had a young man come to my office. He was a returned missionary—one of my former missionaries. He was very sober when he came in. He said, "President Packer, I have a very serious problem. Can I talk to you?" I asked him, "So you want counsel?" And he said, "Well, yes, that is what I have come for."

Then he began to tell me about going to BYU and coming from his mission. He met a beautiful Latter-day Saint girl. They had been courting for a year and a half, and she was an ideal Latter-day Saint girl.

He said, "I've got to decide whether I should marry this girl or I've got to look elsewhere. I've just been spending too much time in this courtship." He extolled her virtues and then he said, "There is only one thing wrong with all of this." I said, "What's that?" And he said, "We just don't seem to like one another." He said, "We're miserable when we're together, and we're miserable when we're apart." And he continued, again describing her as the perfect Latter-day Saint girl, "President Packer, you tell me that it is all right to marry her and we'll schedule the marriage. You tell me that I shouldn't, and I won't. I've come for that counsel."

Then I asked if he follows counsel. He said, "Yes."

So here is my counsel. "You go home this weekend, and you go to your father. You get alone with your father and tell him what you told me; and you do what he says. That is my counsel to you."

He turned pale and said, "But Brother Packer, this is a serious problem." I told him I had no other counsel for him.

That next weekend he went home to his father. Incidentally, his father is a bishop, but even given these circumstances the young man hesitated to go to his father. So he told his father about this courtship. She was everything his mind said he ought to want, except they didn't get along. Then a wise father gave him some counsel that I can pass along.

"David," said the father, "do you know what is wrong with this courtship? Every time you go out with this girl you go just as though you were going to buy a horse. You have a set of specifications, and you are testing and looking and seeing. You're measuring every particular to see whether she will measure up and be good enough and meet all of *your* specifications." This wise father said, "David, the thing that is wrong with you is that you are selfish. If you would worry half as much about whether *you* were meeting *her* specifications as you worry about whether she met yours, you'd find your answer."

Not long after this we gathered in the sealing room of the temple to seal this fine young man and this lovely young Latter-day Saint woman together as husband and wife for time and for all eternity. And there began, in that counsel with that father, a beautiful, romantic, poetic, star-filled courtship because the principles of unselfishness had been observed.

22

TEACHING CHILDREN TITHING

In the Church children are taught the principle of tithing, but it is at home that the principle is applied. At home even young children can be shown how to figure a tithe and how it is paid.

One time President and Sister Harold B. Lee were in our home. Sister Lee put a handful of pennies on a table before our young son. She had him slide the shiny ones to one side and said, "These are your tithing; these belong to the Lord. The others are yours to keep." He thoughtfully looked from one pile to the other and then said, "Don't you have any more dirty ones?" That was when the real teaching moment began!

23

TO CALL INSTEAD OF INVITE

When I was a young man, Elder Spencer W. Kimball came to our conference and he told this experience. When he was a stake president in Safford, Arizona, there was a vacancy in the office of superintendent of Young Men in the stake, as the office was then called. He left his office one day, went a few steps down the street, and had a conversation with the owner of a business. He said, "Jack, how would you like to be superintendent of the stake Young Men's organization?"

Jack replied: "Aw, Spencer, you don't mean me."

Spencer replied, "Of course I do. You get along well with the youth." He tried to convince him, but the man turned him down.

Later in the day, after smoldering with his failure and finally remembering what Jacob had said in the Book of Mormon—"having obtained mine errand from the Lord" (Jacob 1:17)—he returned to Jack. Calling him "Brother" and by his last name, he said, "We have a vacancy in a stake office. My counselors and I have discussed it; we've prayed about it for some time. Sunday we knelt down together and asked the Lord for inspiration about who should be called to that position. We received the inspiration that you should be called. As a servant of the Lord, I am here to deliver that call."

Jack said, "Well, Spencer, if you are going to put it that way . . ."

"Well, I am putting it that way."

You know the result. It helps to follow the proper order of things, even the unwritten order.

24

"WHY ARE YOU SITTING HERE?"

Some years ago Sister Packer and I got off the plane in Chicago, where a stopover was scheduled. We had the "occupied" cards in our seats, and, though the plane wasn't full, when we got back on the plane we noticed that a man was sitting in the seat next to me. I was irritated. I have a little trouble with cigarette smoke, and I thought he'd sit and blow smoke on me all the way. I glanced back and saw all the empty seats in back of us and wondered why he didn't take one of those seats.

He was a fine-looking young man, and as missionaries will, I was soon engaged in a conversation with him. It wasn't long before I could tell he didn't smoke. We had a visit. I asked him who he was, where he was going, and so forth—that always invites the inquiry and begins the conversation. As soon as I mentioned I was a member of the Church, he said, "Oh, my wife is a member of your church. She just became a member."

Then we had an interesting conversation in which he

started talking about "our" bishop and "our" this and "our" that. I finally asked, "Why aren't you a member?"

Immediately his countenance changed. "I can't," he said, "I would give anything if I could, but I can't. It isn't anything personal with me, but it relates to other people. I just can't. There is something that has to be answered; I've just prayed that I could talk with somebody. I thought maybe of talking with one of the leaders or somebody about this question."

I asked, "Why do you suppose you're sitting in this seat?"

"What do you mean?" he responded.

I said, "Look back there." He glanced over, and I added, "See all those empty seats. Why do you suppose you're sitting here? Was that an accident?"

So we began to talk. We talked about the pioneer trail, and I talked to him about the scriptures, and for some reason I said, "Let me give you a sample of what's in the Book of Mormon." I read to him chapter forty-two of Alma as we rode along in the plane. I just read it and he listened. Then we got off in Salt Lake City. He had some business there and was going on to the West Coast.

I asked him, "Has your wife ever been to a general conference of the Church?"

He replied, "No."

I said, "That would be a marvelous thing."

"Well," he responded, "we can't come."

I said, "Well, in case something should happen to change that, we'll be staying at Hotel Utah." Then we parted.

The next week, when general conference came, on Friday night near midnight I got a call from California. It was this same young man. "We're leaving right now," he said. "We're going to drive all night to come to conference."

So we met this couple—a very lovely wife and a fine

young man, a young professional engineer—and made arrangements so they could get into a session or two of conference, and then Sunday afternoon they came over to my office.

He told me, "I don't need to go into that problem anymore. It's solved, and the next time I see you . . ."

I knew what he was going to say, but I interrupted him and said, "You'll hold the priesthood!"

He said, "That's right."

Then he told me something more about our flight together. "Do you know why I sat by you in Chicago? I was assigned that seat. Normally they only assign seats at the place of flight origin, and I was irritated that they gave me a seat assignment. I walked on the plane thinking, 'I won't sit there.' But then I thought, 'Well, there must be some reason for it.' That was the seat I was assigned to, and that's why I was sitting by you."

Well, I don't know what his problem was, but the answer was in the Book of Mormon. Teach them, if they are to keep the faith, to read the revealed word.

25

THE SPIRIT OF REVELATION

During World War II, having graduated from flight training and received my silver wings, I was stationed at Langley Field, Virginia, as copilot on a selected B-24 bomber crew. My older brother, then Colonel Leon C. Packer, was stationed at the Pentagon in Washington, D.C. I was able to spend a few days with him before shipping out.

He had had much experience with the B-24 bomber, and he told me of the things he had learned. Few of these planes that made raids over southern Europe ever returned. Leon crash-landed more than once.

As we visited, he told me how he was able to hold himself together under fire. He said, "I have a favorite hymn"—— and he named it—"and when things got rough I would sing it silently to myself, and there would come a faith and an assurance that kept me on course." He sent me off to combat with that lesson.

In the spring of 1945 I was able to test the lesson Leon had taught me those months before.

The war in the Pacific ended before we reached the Philippines, and we were ordered to Japan.

One day we flew out of Atsugi airfield near Yokohama in a B-17 bomber bound for Guam to pick up a beacon light. After nine hours in the air, we let down through the clouds to find ourselves hopelessly lost. Our radio was out. We were, as it turned out, in a typhoon.

Flying just above the ocean, we began a search pattern. In that desperate situation, I remembered the words of my brother. I learned that you can pray and even sing without making a sound.

After some time we pulled up over a line of rocks jutting out of the water. Could they be part of the chain of the Mariana Islands? We followed them. Soon Tinian Island loomed ahead, and we landed with literally seconds of fuel in the tank. As we headed down the runway, the engines one by one stopped.

I learned that both prayer and music can be very silent and very personal.

Now, while that experience was dramatic, the greater value of Leon's lesson came later in everyday life when I faced the same temptations young people and children face now.

As the years passed I found that, while it was not easy, I could control my thoughts if I made a place for them to go. You can replace thoughts of temptation, anger, disappointment, or fear with better thoughts—with music.

26

LOVE BEYOND SELF

I recall on one occasion, when I was returning from seminary to my home for lunch, I drove in and my wife met me in the driveway. I could tell by the expression on her face that something was wrong. "Cliff has been killed," she said. "They want you to come over."

As I hastened around the corner to where Cliff lived with his wife and four sons and his little daughter, I saw Cliff lying in the middle of the highway with a blanket over him. The ambulance was just pulling away with little Colleen. Cliff had been on his way out to the farm and had stopped to cross the street to take little Colleen to her mother, who waited on the opposite curb. But the child, as children will, broke from her father's hand and slipped into the street. A large truck was coming. Cliff jumped from the curb and pushed his little daughter from the path of the truck—but he wasn't soon enough.

A few days later I had the responsibility of speaking at the funeral of Cliff and little Colleen. Someone said, "What a terrible waste. Certainly he ought to have stayed on the curb.

He knew the child might have died. But he had four sons and a wife to provide for. What a pathetic waste!" I estimated that the individual never had had the experience of loving someone more than he loved himself.

To you who are young, this experience of loving someone more than you love yourself can come, insofar as I know, through the exercise of the power of creation. Through it you become really Christian, and you know, as few others know, what the word *Father* means when it is spoken of in the scriptures; and you feel some of the love and concern that He has for us. You may experience some of the remorse and sorrow that must be His if we fail to accept all that is beautiful and praiseworthy and of good report in this world.

27

NATURE KNOWS

Some years ago my father-in-law owned a ranch in Wyoming. Our children worked there during the summers. We would always go up there for the 24th of July celebration that this little, tiny ward held up in the mountains. They had some homespun activities that we found delightful. Among them was something a little unusual.

They would cut down an aspen tree and take off the bark. Now, an aspen tree without bark is a very slick thing. They would drive a nail into the top of it and put a five-dollar bill on the nail with a clothespin. Then they would set the trunk of the tree in the ground securely and anyone who could shinny up the post could have the five-dollar bill.

For three years in a row our little daughter won. She would outdo the ranch boys by shinnying up the pole, apparently without much effort.

When she moved into her teens, her father, who had watched the boys, noticed that she had noticed that the boys had begun to notice. It might be time for a lesson.

That year as we were going to the picnic, I had a moment

to be alone with her, and I said, "This time I think you won't win the five dollars."

She looked at me in surprise, because it had been so easy before. "Don't you think I can do it?" she asked.

"Oh, I know you can do it," I said. "I just wonder if you should."

Our girls have always paid attention to what their father has said. After she had a chance to think about it, can you see her coming to me and squeezing my hand and saying, "Thanks, Daddy"?

Somehow I have never been interested, as a father, in having our daughters reduce themselves to equality with men. It is against their natures. That would be to yield some heights God intended that they should reach.

There are some things women, by nature, can do so much better than men. There are some spiritual virtues that women must protect for men—or great, very, very great will be the cost.

28

PUTTING TOGETHER A BOY

One winter, our sixteen-year-old found in the neighborhood, under a pile of snow, a 1948 Ford tractor—sort of. He asked if he could buy it. It had stood, I think, for fifteen years without being used. It was rusted almost away. But he saw something there and I saw something in him seeing something there.

So, with another old tractor, we dragged it through the snowdrifts home to the shop and later to the high school shop. There a shop teacher and our son worked evening after evening to restore this tractor. Every few days it came again! "Dad, I found out that we've got to buy this or that." Strangely enough, he could find it. He got his driver's license midway, and so off to Heber City he was for this part or somewhere else for that part. I, too, went with him to more than one city looking through junkyards for old tractor parts.

Then as the bills mounted, someone who knew made the observation that that tractor was a very expensive investment. Perhaps a mistake. I thought he made the mistake. He thought we were putting together a tractor. I thought we were putting together a boy.

Somewhere in the middle of this the tractor wouldn't work, and the shop teacher couldn't find the problem. So we made a call to a long since retired eighty-four-year-old man who spent his life with tractors. He showed up one evening and pointed out this and that to help my boy, and then he was off again.

Eventually the tractor was assembled and in good working condition. A victory and a lesson for a boy.

29

REINFORCING PRAYER

Here is a lesson drawn from a little girl who reported to her mother that her brother was setting traps for birds. She didn't like it at all.

"He won't catch any birds in his trap, will he, Mother?" she asked. "I have prayed about it and asked Heavenly Father to protect the birds. He won't catch anything, will he, Mother?" Becoming more positive, she said, "I know he won't catch anything, because I have prayed about it."

The mother asked, "How can you be sure he won't catch anything?"

Then came a meaningful addition. "He won't catch anything because, after I said my prayers, I went out and kicked that old trap all to pieces."

30

SELF-RELIANCE

We have all been taught that revelation is available to each of us individually. The question I'm most often asked about revelation is, "How do I know when I have received it? I've prayed about it and fasted over this problem and prayed about it and prayed about it, and I still don't quite know what to do. How can I really tell whether I'm being inspired so I won't make a mistake?"

First, do you go to the Lord with a problem and ask Him to make your decision for you? Or do you work and meditate and pray and then make a decision yourself? Measure the problem against what you know to be right and wrong, and then make the decision. Then ask Him if the decision is right or if it is wrong. Remember what He said to Oliver Cowdery about working it out in your mind.

If we foolishly ask our bishop or branch president or the Lord to make a decision for us, there's precious little self-reliance in that. Think what it costs every time you have somebody else make a decision for you.

I think I should mention one other thing, and I hope this

won't be misunderstood. We often find young people who will pray with great exertion over matters that they are free to decide for themselves. Suppose, if you will, that a couple had money available to build a house. Suppose they had prayed endlessly over whether they should build an Early American style, a ranch style, modern-style architecture, or perhaps a Mediterranean style. Has it ever occurred to you that perhaps the Lord just plain doesn't care? Let them build what they want to build. It's their choice. In many things we can do just what we want.

Now, there are some things He cares about very much. If you're going to build that house, then be honest and pay for the material that goes into it and do a decent job of building it. When you move into it, live righteously in it. Those are the things that count.

On occasions I've had to counsel people that the Lord would probably quite willingly approve the thing they intend to do, even when it's something they want to do. It's strange when they come and almost feel guilty about doing something they want to do, even when it's righteous. The Lord is very generous with the freedom He gives us. The more we learn to follow the right, the more we are spiritually self-reliant, the more our freedom and our independence are affirmed.

31

SHE WAS A MOTHER

When I was just a youngster in school there was an epidemic of impetigo, a skin infection. In those days there was not the medication we have now, and the best that could be done for it was to have it painted with purple medicine. Everybody knew who had impetigo if they were doctoring it.

In my school was a family of little youngsters. There was a sadness in their home, and they didn't have the attention of a mother. The impetigo that first infected their hands and then their faces soon was on their bodies. They came to school in such clothing as they had.

My mother was a room mother then, a parent-teacher assignment. The principal asked if she would go to the home and use her influence to persuade the family to keep the children home, because there was the probability that they would be carrying the infection to other children. My mother's heart wouldn't let her do that. I remember her telling us to bring the children home with us.

I remember that for weeks we'd bring those other little children home and Mother would bathe them and doctor

them and put on them our underclothing and send them
home; and I can remember my mother with a bottle of disin-
fectant scrubbing for hours and boiling clothing and underclothing against the possibility of her family becoming
infected. She was a mother.

*Recently I heard a speaker in sacrament meeting complain
that he could not understand why his grandchildren always
spoke of going to Grandma's house, never to Grandpa's house.
I solved that great mystery for him: Grandpas don't bake pies!*
(From "For Time and All Eternity," ENSIGN,
November 1993, p. 22)

32

"I A PERSON"

Some time ago I watched two young sons wrestling on a rug before the fireplace. As the tempo of their play became strained, as the laughter was near turning to tears, I worked my foot gently between the two contestants and separated them with the gentle admonition—"Hey there, you two monkeys, you'd better quiet down."

The older of the two, a four-year-old, sat up with his little arms folded and looked up with a seriousness that let me know that his little-boy feelings had been injured. And then he advised me with some emphasis—"I not a monkey, Daddy! I a person."

The youngster's declaration, "I a person," came with such fervor that I pondered on the meaning of his words, "I a person," which came with more certainty from this little boy than from many a learned scientist or philosopher.

There flooded into my mind an appreciation of how much I loved these little boys—how much I hoped for them and how I would do for them.

No doubt every father has at one time or another been

overwhelmed with the realization that his little boy or his little girl was indeed a person! And to most has come, almost as a revelation, the fact that this little person—for whose material and spiritual destiny a father is responsible—is a child of God.

33

WHO SUPPORTS WHOM?

After the Saturday evening session of a quarterly conference, a stake president advised me that he had arranged for a member of his stake, a former seminary student of mine, to drive me to his home. "He wanted to visit with you, very much," he said, "and this will give him an opportunity to see you alone and I will meet you at my house."

I was happy to see Ray again. I'm always happy to see my former seminary students still active in the Church. He told me there was an important reason why he wanted to see me alone. He had just been called as the stake superintendent of one of the auxiliaries and he really wanted to do an excellent job, but there was a serious problem. He knew that I could help with it, and that was the purpose for our interview.

"Our stake president just doesn't support us," he said. "We just don't get the support from our stake presidency. While you are meeting with them, would you do something so that they will give us their support? You don't know how hard it is to try to run an organization when even the stake presidency doesn't support you."

I listened very carefully, and then I said, "Ray, haven't you got things backwards?" He asked what I meant, and I asked the question, "Who is supposed to be supporting whom?" We drove for a few miles, and he was very thoughtful, and then he said, "I think I've found the answer to our problem." And I added by way of explanation: "I wince a little when I hear an auxiliary leader in the stake say: 'We have a great stake president; we've never had such a fine stake president. He really supports Primary (or Young Men, Sunday School, or Relief Society). We've never had priesthood leaders who supported us like these do.'

"Now, I know that sounds positive, but what a difference it makes when that same spirit of cooperation is spoken in these words: 'We have a great stake president and dedicated priesthood leaders. What an honor it is to lead an auxiliary organization in support of priesthood leaders and priesthood programs like these.'"

34

LATTER-DAY SAINT
INFLUENCE ENDURES

One Sunday, Sister Packer and I were returning from an assignment in Europe, the last three days of which were spent in St. Petersburg, Russia. There we met the missionaries with the members and attended a fireside for members and investigators. We held two days of meetings with the leaders of the priesthood of the district and the branches there. While that is a different world, it is the same world. I was reminded of how important the little things are in our lives.

We were invited to the office of Vladimir P. Yakovlev, who is the deputy mayor of St. Petersburg, to have lunch with him. The first thing he said through an interpreter was: "You don't need to tell me about your church or about your beliefs. I know about you, your people. Thirty years ago," he said, "I was on a cultural exchange in Pittsburg, Pennsylvania, and I stayed for two months in the home of Timothy and Dorthea Smith. I saw them and their family. I went to the meetings with them."

He said, "I just read the reports." It happens, incidentally, that in that city of five million, among his other duties he has the responsibility for advising on all matters relating to religion. He said, "The reports show that you are an honest people. When you say you will do something, you will do it. When you say that you will not do something, you will not do it. You are people who can be trusted."

I told him we would try to find Timothy and Dorthea Smith. I haven't as yet had the opportunity. He said he would like to get in touch with them again.

Who would have supposed that thirty years ago in that chance encounter members of the Church, just behaving themselves, would influence a man who now is in a very crucial position to affect the onrolling of the work of the Lord in that great city which only a short time ago was behind the Iron Curtain?

35

THE SPIRIT OF SERVICE

Over the years I have watched one dear sister give service far beyond any calling to teach or lead in the Church. She sees a need and serves; not "Call me if you need help," but "Here I am; what can I do?" She does so many small things, like holding someone's child in a meeting or taking a child to school who has missed the bus. She always looks for new faces at church and steps forward to make them welcome.

Her husband knows that when they attend a ward social he can generally count on her saying, "Why don't you go along home. I see they are a little short on help to clear up and do the dishes."

He came home one evening to find her putting the furniture back in place. That morning she had the feeling that she should see how an elderly sister with a heart condition was managing a wedding breakfast for a grandchild who had come from out of state to be married in the temple.

She found the woman sitting alone at the church, in despair, surrounded by the things she had brought in preparation. Somehow there had been a double booking of the hall. In a few hours the guests would arrive. Whatever could she do?

This attentive sister took the older sister home with her and put her down to rest. Then she went to work moving the furniture around. When the guests arrived, a beautiful wedding breakfast was ready to be served.

She learned that spirit of service from her mother. The spirit of service is best taught at home.

36

A TEACHER'S INFLUENCE

Today I reflect on the influence of a teacher that I knew more than fifty years ago. As is often the case, the influence of that teacher did not center on the subject he taught. Dr. Schaefer was a professor of mathematics at Washington State University at Pullman, Washington. He was quite unimpressive in appearance. I don't remember his first name, but I shall never forget the first thing he said the first day we met.

It was during World War II. We were in pilot training and had been sent to the university for what we were told would be a crash course in meteorology, weather, navigation, physics, aerodynamics, and other technical subjects. We thought the title "crash course" was not very encouraging to student pilots. The word *intense* would have been better.

The pressure was enormous because those who failed the course would be washed out of the pilot program. I was in competition with cadets, many of whom had been to college; some of them had had some advanced training, while I had barely escaped from high school.

Dr. Schaefer was to take us from basic mathematics

through calculus in just a matter of weeks. I thought it was hopeless—until that first few minutes in the first class. He began the class with this announcement: "While many of you have had some college, even advanced courses in what we are to study, it will be my purpose to teach the beginners. I am asking those of you who know the subject to be patient while I teach the basics to those who do not." Encouraged by what he said and more by how he taught, I was able to pass that course with reasonable ease. It might otherwise have been impossible.

When I decided to become a teacher, Dr. Schaefer's example inspired me to try to the best of my ability to teach basic, simple truths in the most understandable way. I have learned how very difficult it is to simplify.

Years after the war, I returned to Washington State University and found Dr. Schaefer. He, of course, did not remember me. I was just one of many hundreds of cadets in his classes. I thanked him for what he had taught me. The math and calculus had long since faded away, but not his example as a teacher.

37

A WARD FAMILY

I was at a funeral. A mother of seven children, the oldest eleven, the youngest two, was taken in death in a matter of hours. The funeral was touching. We saw the little family come in, the father carrying the two-year-old. Early in the service, as little youngsters are wont to do, she became restless and soon was whimpering and calling for her mama.

It should have been an experience of agony. But it was not. There was no anguish there either. It was an exalting experience in many ways. Great faith was shown.

Soon the little three-year-old was restless likewise. I noticed the father nod to someone in the row behind them. A lovely lady moved forward and took the little youngsters to comfort them, and then took them out into the foyer, where she could tend them. That was the Relief Society. I thought how important that was now to this little family.

I asked that father and husband a day or two later what they were going to do. He explained that the family was helping. The grandmother was there, and, of course, the family should help. But the responsibility of these seven children would be too much for the grandmother. Then he said, "But we have all the other women standing by." They belong to a family—a ward family—and the sisterhood part of it is the Relief Society.

The Church will grow until it fills the whole earth.
At once it will remain no bigger than the ward.
(From "The Bishop and His Counselors,"
ENSIGN, May 1999, p. 63)

38

LEADERS KEEP CONFIDENCES

Years ago in one of our Church schools, a teacher was summarily dismissed. The general explanation given did not satisfy his colleagues.

A delegation went to the office of the president and demanded that he be reinstated. The president refused. He offered no further explanation. The delegation concluded, therefore, that the president had acted for "political reasons," for he was known to have some deep philosophical differences with that teacher.

The teacher (and this is frequently the case) took the part of a mistreated soul. His actions encouraged his colleagues in their protest.

The truth, known to the members of the Church Board of Education, was that the teacher had been dismissed for some very serious misconduct. Should all be made public, it would be doubtful that he could be reemployed as a teacher.

The president, however, had some faith. If things were not noised about, the teacher might, through repentance and restitution, make himself again worthy to teach—perhaps even in the Church school system.

This president generously took much criticism, even abuse, over a long period of time. He felt that the good of a family and the rehabilitation of a teacher was more important than his own professional reputation for the moment.

I was inspired by his example. It has been repeated a thousand times or more in the wards and stakes of the Church.

Often actions of bishops and stake presidents and others are misread by people who are not in a position to know the full truth. Neither the bishop nor the member he is judging is obliged to confide in us. The bishop must keep confidences.

When all is said and done, in most cases, it is clearly none of our business anyway.

Often someone will not go to his bishop with a problem. He wants to see a General Authority instead. He says the bishop will talk—for what about the time when someone in the ward went to him and soon everyone knew about the problem?

Follow these cases through, as I have done, and you will probably find that, first, the member confided in her neighbor who didn't know what to counsel her. Then she talked it over with her best friend, and then her sister, and received conflicting advice. Finally, her husband was told by the man he rides with that they'd better see the bishop.

Indeed, it was noised about, but not by the bishop. Bishops keep confidences.

39

LEAVING THE TEAM STANDING

Years ago I served on a stake high council with Emery Wight. For ten years Emery had served as bishop of rural Harper Ward. His wife, Lucille, became our stake Relief Society president.

Lucille told me that one spring morning a neighbor called at her door and asked for Emery. She told him that he was out plowing. The neighbor then spoke with great concern. Earlier that morning he had passed the field and noticed Emery's team of horses standing in a half-finished furrow with the reins draped over the plow. Emery was nowhere in sight. The neighbor thought nothing of it until much later when he passed the field again, and the team had not moved. He climbed the fence and crossed the field to the horses. Emery was nowhere to be found. He hurried to the house to check with Lucille.

Lucille calmly replied, "Oh, don't be alarmed. No doubt someone is in trouble and came to get the bishop."

The image of that team of horses standing for hours in the field symbolizes the dedication of the bishops in the

Church and of the counselors who stand by their side. Every bishop and every counselor, figuratively speaking, leaves his team standing in an unfinished furrow when someone needs help.

40

OBEDIENCE

Let me tell you how one of our sons learned obedience. When he was about deacon age, we went to his grandfather's ranch in Wyoming. He wanted to start breaking a horse he had been given. It had been running wild in the hills.

It took nearly all day to get the herd to the corral and to tie his horse up with a heavy halter and a rope.

I told him that his horse must stay tied there until it settled down; he could talk to it, carefully touch it, but he must not, under any circumstances, untie it.

We finally went in for our supper. He quickly ate and rushed back out to see his horse. Presently I heard him cry out. I knew what had happened. He had untied his horse. He was going to train it to lead. As the horse pulled away from him he instinctively did something I had told him never, never to do. He looped the rope around his wrist to get a better grip.

As I ran from the house, I saw the horse go by. Our boy could not release the rope; he was being pulled with great leaping steps. And then he went down! If the horse had turned to the right, he would have been dragged out the gate and into the hills and would certainly have lost his life. It turned to the left, and for a moment was hung up in a fence corner—just long enough for me to loop the rope around a post and to free my son.

Then came a father-to-son chat! "Son, if you are ever going to control that horse, you will have to use something besides your muscles. The horse is bigger than you are, it is stronger than you are, and it always will be. Someday you may ride your horse if you train it to be obedient, a lesson that you must learn yourself first." He had learned a very valuable lesson.

Two summers later we went again to the ranch to look for his horse. It had been running all winter with the wild herd. We found them in a meadow down by the river. I watched from a hillside as he and his sister moved carefully to the edge of the meadow. The horses moved nervously away. Then he whistled. His horse hesitated, then left the herd and trotted up to them.

My son had learned that there is great power in things that are not seen, such unseen things as obedience. Just as obedience to principle gave him power to train his horse, obedience to the priesthood has taught him to control himself.

41

NOT EVEN A SPARROW

Not too long ago I visited the military cemetery at Margraden in the Netherlands. It is situated in the beautiful, rolling countryside, not far from where the borders of the Netherlands, Belgium, and Germany meet.

Row after row of white crosses fade into the distance. They mark the graves of more than ten thousand American servicemen who died in one major action in World War II. The cemetery is well kept. There is a spirit there. The few visitors you meet are reverent and subdued.

You see an elderly couple moving up and down the rows looking for a marker. It is not too difficult to know that he has recently retired. They have saved money over the years and they are visiting for the first time the grave of their son.

If you see a middle-aged woman standing at a grave, the image in her mind is not of a middle-aged American man but of a young man whom she loved so much and for so short a time before he was taken from her.

He was younger than even her son is, who stands by her side with his wife. The son gets fixed in his mind for the first

time the place where his father is buried. This image somehow becomes the most prominent memory of his father,
because he was such a little fellow when the telegram came
announcing that his father was a casualty.

They leave after a time, and you know that she will put
forth a real but probably futile effort to enjoy something she
never thought she would have, and that is a trip to Europe.

As we wandered among the markers, we could find one
here and there from Santaquin or Scipio, from Garland, or
Logan, or Malad.

There are the graves, also marked, known only to God.
And more touching even than this are the long lists of names
on the large monument, for those who just were gone. They
were there when the battle started, and gone when it ended.

I am not ashamed to admit that those crosses and the few
Stars of David mixed among them become distorted when
you look at them through tears. They seem almost like a large
contingent of men dressed in white uniforms, standing at
attention awaiting the orders of the greatest commander, to
fall out and be about their personal eternal affairs.

I have in mind the other casualties, those whose bodies
have been injured, or whose minds have been broken; those
who languish in hospitals or live a limited life these years
after the hostilities have ceased.

I have in mind also those who have been bereft of a
loved one. The more fortunate among them perhaps know
what happened and when and where he is buried. To those
who have a husband or son still listed just as "missing," I
would offer comfort.

I remind all of us that there is not one of them but that
shall ultimately be accounted for. For the Lord has said that
not even a sparrow should fall, save notice be taken. And no

sacrifice so important as they have made will go unnoticed or unrecorded by Him.

And there are times when He is the only one to whom one can turn for solace when men either will not, or perhaps they cannot, do more to end the long and ceaseless wondering.

I do not think the Lord is quite so hopeless about what's going on in the world as we are. He could put a stop to all of it any moment. But He will not! Not until every player has a chance to meet the test for which we were prepared before the world was, before we came into mortality.

(From "The Mystery of Life," ENSIGN, November 1983, p. 18)

42

ASK THE RIGHT QUESTIONS

Some time ago I had a letter from a group of Latter-day Saint young women at BYU. They had a list of questions they wanted me to answer. I had a hard time. First, I couldn't read the questions; I didn't even know what they meant. I'd never heard of some of the language of the day, so I finally took it home to my teenage boy and he interpreted it for me. So at least I knew then what it was they were trying to get me to answer.

I put the letter on my desk, and I think for nearly a month it would shuffle up to the top and I didn't know what to do with it. I knew I should answer it because you don't not answer letters.

One day I came to Temple Square to perform a sealing ordinance, and there I got the inspiration.

I saw the fine, stalwart, well-framed young man and the lovely, beautiful, feminine bride, and had the privilege of officiating in sealing them together for time and for all eternity. I knew why I hadn't been able to answer that letter. I went back to my office and answered it this way:

Dear Sisters:

You said in your letter of some weeks past that you were preoccupied with these questions and couldn't find an answer, and so you were writing to one of the General Authorities. I apologize for not having answered sooner, but I couldn't, and today I found out why. I couldn't answer, because you asked all the wrong questions.

Every question you asked was a question asking for license and liberty. You wanted to know how far you should go toward the precipice of immorality and transgression, without falling over. If you really had the spirit, the right spirit, you would have been asking questions on how you could stay completely away from any possibility of falling over that precipice.

Sisters, in your youth, as you prepare, learn to ask the right kind of questions. Sister Packer is right when she says that "there are no 'have to's' in the gospel of Jesus Christ, they are all 'get to's.'"

43

A LESSON ABOUT JUDGING

Years ago I learned a lesson about judging. I was a city councilman in Brigham City and was also on the stake high council. Late one night I was returning home from a high council meeting, pondering on what had happened there.

There was a red light and a siren. I was given a ticket for going forty-five miles an hour in a thirty-mile-an-hour zone. I accepted the ticket without protest, for I had not been paying attention.

The city judge was always in his office very early, and I went to get the matter settled before going to teach seminary the next day.

The judge had recently made a request for some new furniture. It rested with me, as a councilman, to approve it and sign the voucher.

He looked at my ticket and smiled, saying, "There have, on occasions, been exceptions made."

I told him that in view of my position he was obliged to treat me like any other citizen. Reluctantly he consented.

"The going rate is a dollar a mile. That will be fifteen dollars."

I paid the fine.

Two nights later one councilman reported in a meeting of the city council that he had fired a policeman. When the mayor asked the cause, he was told, and I quote: "Well, he was always arresting the wrong people."

Later the councilman explained that there had been vandalism in the city. Late at night someone had gone down Forest Street in a recreation vehicle and snapped off all the young trees. There had been damage in the cemetery also.

The councilman had tried over a period of weeks to get the police to patrol the city at night. Where were they? He found they were hiding behind signboards waiting for some unwary motorist. One young officer just did not seem to learn, and so he had been dismissed.

He, then, was the man who gave a traffic ticket to a city councilman. Two days later he was dismissed. And the cause, stated in a city council meeting, with several delegations as witness: "He was always arresting the wrong people."

Do you think he could be convinced that I did not cause him to be fired?

Had I known of it, I may have prevented his dismissal, because of the appearances.

Appearances, however, convicted me of unworthy use of influence.

44

GOD'S RULES PREVAIL

Many years ago I was one of the supervisors of the seminary. We had received word from a stake president that a new seminary teacher was having a great deal of difficulty. He was inexperienced, and in that high school at that time they had kind of a rough bunch of youngsters.

I walked into the seminary, and I could tell which class he was trying to teach because I could hear, and it was not the teacher I heard. They were very noisy. I opened the door. Some of them were standing up. I was able to slip in and take a seat in the back of the class as he struggled to teach the youngsters the gospel. But they were not interested in what he had to say.

After a few minutes I felt so sorry for him. I understood, because I had been in that position. Presently he saw me and stopped mid-sentence. So I walked to the front of the room and said, "Let me try." The class was quiet for just a minute, just because I was a stranger. I asked if anyone in the class was on the football team. A fine young athlete stood up, and I said, "When were you elected to the football team?"

He said, "Well, I wasn't elected."

I said, "How did you get on the team, then?"

He said, "I had to prepare myself and try out."

I said, "I don't think that is fair. I don't think that is the way you ought to pick a football team. Why don't you all take turns, just go through the class and take turns being on the team?"

He did not think that would work very well. The rest of the class did not think so either. I asked if there was a member of the cheerleaders, and a lovely young woman stood up. I said, "When were you elected to be one of the cheerleaders?"

She said, "I wasn't elected."

I said, "Well, how did you get to be one?"

She said, "We had to try out, and we had to work. We had to commit ourselves to do certain things, to practice, and we had to say we were going to invest a lot of time."

To make a point, I said, "I don't think this school is fair. I think all of the girls ought to be on the cheerleading team if they want to. Just take turns."

Pretty soon there was an argument going on between me and the students. They were insisting that they would not have a very good football team if they worked the way I was proposing. I asked the football player if he had to follow any rules.

He said, "It is all rules."

I said, "That is no fun! Why do you have so many rules? Why do you take all of the fun out of it?"

We talked for a little while. I kept telling them that in order to be fair, you should not have any rules. Everybody should be equal.

They were very vigorous in trying to convince me you

needed rules; and that if you are going to do anything worth-while, there were going to be restrictions and commitments. Finally, they made a believer out of me.

Of course, the next thing I said was: "It is just like that in the Church. Do you think our Father in Heaven should be fair? Well, some people think He is not very fair. When the Lord was upon the earth, He made a statement. He said: 'Except a man be born of water and of the Spirit, he cannot enter into the kingdom of God' [John 3:5]."

So He had made rules. To grow we must follow rules in life.

Some are so near spiritual death that they must be spoonfed of the broth of fellowship.
(From "Feed My Sheep," ENSIGN, May 1984, p. 42)

45

WHEN THE SPIRIT LEFT

As a mission president I received some instruction by revelation and I didn't follow it. I learned a lesson that I have never forgotten. I hope it never needs to be repeated.

It centered on an organizational change. It centered on the counselor that should be released. Logic said no because he was experienced; he had served three other mission presidents. He knew everything about the mission. We called a priesthood leadership meeting at conference. He said the brethren wouldn't come. I said they would. He said: "No. Those Vermonters won't come to meetings like that." I knew the Church was stalled if they did not, so I called the meeting for a Saturday afternoon, a priesthood leadership meeting. Brother Dunn and I and the other counselor went up to Vermont. There were about fifty people invited. We outnumbered them. So my counselor was right—they wouldn't come to a meeting.

I knew if I followed the counsel of this counselor any longer, the mission was stalled. But how could I release him? He was such a wonderful man. A patriarchal man. He was such a help, such a resource. Then, the Spirit left me. For about a week I went through hell because there was nothing there.

Finally, one day in the office, I put on my coat and hat, left the office without calling my wife to say I wouldn't be home for lunch, then drove ninety miles. I found the counselor and told him that I had come to release him. I said, "Can you accept the release?" He said, "Well, why?" I said, "Because it's right. Can you accept that?" He said, "Well, yes." Meaning no.

I will never forget when I left him. I had prayed all this time, asking the questions, "If I release him, who should I replace him with?" No answer would come.

As I got in the car after releasing him, the Spirit of the Lord flooded in. I knew who should be the counselor. The Lord would speak to me again.

I was pleased when the stake was later organized that he was called as the patriarch.

46

WE HAVE BEEN CALLED

On one occasion I was in the office of President Henry D. Moyle when a phone call he had placed earlier in the day came through. After greeting the caller, he said, "I wonder if your business affairs would bring you into Salt Lake City sometime in the near future? I would like to meet with you and your wife, for I have a matter of some importance that I would like to discuss with you."

Well, though it was many miles away, that man all of a sudden discovered that his business would bring him to Salt Lake City the very next morning. I was in the same office the following day when President Moyle announced to this man that he had been called to preside over one of the missions of the Church. "Now," he said, "we don't want to rush you into this decision. Would you call me in a day or two, as soon as you are able to make a determination as to your feelings concerning this call?"

The man looked at his wife and she looked at him, and without saying a word there was that silent conversation between husband and wife, and that gentle, almost imperceptible nod. He turned back to President Moyle and said, "Well, President, what is there to say? What could we tell you in a few days that we couldn't tell you now? We have been called. What answer is there? Of course we will respond to the call."

Then President Moyle said rather gently, "Well, if you feel that way about it, actually there is some urgency about this matter. I wonder if you could be prepared to leave by ship from the West Coast on the 14th of March."

The man gulped, for that was just eleven days away. He glanced at his wife. There was another silent conversation, and he said, "Yes, President, we can meet that appointment."

"What about your business?" said the President. "What about your grain elevator? What about your livestock? What about your other holdings?"

"I don't know," said the man, "but we will make arrangements somehow. All of those things will be all right."

Such is the great miracle that we see repeated over and over, day after day, among the faithful. And yet there are many among us who have not the faith to respond to the call or to sustain those who have been so called.

47

THE BISHOP IS IN CHARGE

I received a letter from a brother who was greatly bothered because he was not called to office properly. He accepted the call and was willing to serve, but he said his bishop did not consult his wife first and otherwise did not handle it properly.

When I responded to him, I tried to teach him something of the unwritten order of things as it relates to being a little patient with how things are done in the Church. In the first section of the Doctrine and Covenants, the Lord admonished every man to "speak in the name of God the Lord, even the Savior of the world" (D&C 1:20). I pointed out to him that he may one day be a bishop, overburdened with problems in the ward and with an extra burden of personal cares, and suggested that he give now what he would appreciate receiving then.

Another point of order: Bishops should not yield the arrangement of meetings to members. They should not yield the arrangement for funerals or missionary farewells to families. It is not the proper order of things for members or families to expect to decide who will speak and for how long.

Suggestions are in order, of course, but the bishop should not turn the meeting over to them. We are worried about the drift that is occurring in our meetings.

Funerals could and should be the most spiritually impressive. They are becoming informal family reunions in front of ward members. Often the Spirit is repulsed by humorous experiences or jokes when the time could be devoted to teaching the things of the Spirit, even the sacred things.

When the family insists that several family members speak in a funeral, we hear about the deceased instead of about the Atonement, the Resurrection, and the comforting promises revealed in the scriptures. Now, it's all right to have a family member speak at a funeral, but if they do, their remarks should be in keeping with the spirit of the meeting.

48

SONGS MADE SPIRITUAL

O n one occasion Sister Packer and I were in New Hampshire to speak before the leaders of the Federated Women's Clubs of that state, to conclude their several days' convention on the theme, "Spotlight on Youth—Religion." A convert to the Church, Sister Buswell, had been asked to sing a solo, a final number in the program. She was introduced as a member of the Church. Difficult numbers were easily within range of her well-trained voice, but she stood before the audience and said: "The little children in our Church love to sing. Would you like to hear a medley of songs that are favorite to them, and to the grown-ups, too?" Then she reverently sang a hymn from the Primary songbook of that time, "The Light Divine."

> The light of God rests on the face of brook and flower
>   and tree,
> And kindles in our happy hearts the hope of things to be.
> Father, let thy light divine shine on us we pray,
> Touch our eyes that we may see; teach us to obey.

> *Ours the sacred mission is to bear thy message far.*
> *The light of faith is in our hearts, truth our guiding star.*
> (*Hymns*, no. 305)

As her beautiful voice re-echoed through that hall, a warmth of spirit and emotion flooded into the room. It was a spiritual experience.

She might have chosen other numbers—one perhaps particularly suited to demonstrate for the admiration of those present the quality and capacity of her voice, and the excellence of her training. So often our leaders in music feel the necessity, feel responsible, to "up-grade" and introduce "culture" into our worship services by performing music that is either secular or sectarian, chosen solely because it demonstrates their ability, but is not in keeping with the spirit of the gospel. Such music has an important place—but not in our worship services.

Someone will now say that I don't know much about music. To this I quickly confess. I do know, however, when the Spirit of the Lord is present; and that Spirit rarely yields itself to music that is merely well performed or dignified, any more than it is called forth by the speech of the world, however articulate it might be.

The simplicity and the reverence with which Sister Buswell sang that simple children's hymn caused something spiritual to happen. She continued with another children's hymn, and then, before concluding with a single verse of "O My Father," she sang almost militantly another favorite hymn:

> *Shall the youth of Zion falter*
> *In defending truth and right?*
> *While the enemy assaileth,*
> *Shall we shrink or shun the fight?*

> *While we know the pow'rs of darkness*
> *Seek to thwart the work of God,*
> *Shall the children of the promise*
> *Cease to grasp the iron rod?*
> (Hymns, no. 254)

We need more Sister Buswells in this Church—those who have the inspiration at the appropriate moment to stay in gospel context, not because they cannot equal the world on its own terms, but because they are not ashamed of the gospel of Jesus Christ, for it is the power of God unto salvation (see Romans 1:16).

The words of the simple hymn she sang are in themselves a prayer, with which I close:

> *Father, let thy light divine shine on us, we pray.*
> *Touch our eyes that we may see; teach us to obey.*
> *Ours the sacred mission is to bear thy message far.*
> *The light of faith is in our hearts, truth our guiding star.*

49

"You Are Their Strength"

When I was president of a mission in New England, we had missionaries who were two thousand miles away from mission headquarters, in St. John, Newfoundland. On one occasion I was there interviewing a missionary who was very unsettled.

He was younger than his nineteen years, and in the interview, after talking about his problems, I said, "Elder, do you feel all right?"

He said, "Yes," (which meant no) and I said, "What's the matter, Elder?"

He said, "You're going to go away. I feel all right now, while you are here, but you're going to go away."

I said, "But my assistants come to visit you on occasion."

"Yes," he said, "but they always go away."

"You have zone leaders," I said. "Don't they check on you regularly?"

"Yes, briefly, but they go away," he said. "And then I'm alone again." He said that he felt so alone.

It occurred to me then that I had not taught him the thing that is critical to know in this Church and kingdom.

And so I said, "Elder, didn't you know that when we are gone and you are here, you are to these around you as we are to you. You are their strength."

He pondered on that for a long time and said, "I didn't know that."

Then I said, "Elder, will you be all right?"

He said, "President, I'll be all right, now."

50

A "Chance" Memory

I recall an experience I had when I was supervising the missions in western Europe. We needed a mission president with a certain language proficiency. Several names were brought forward, but none of them seemed to be right. Then one of the Brethren remembered that he had met a man—I think it was in Korea—several years before, a member of the Church who was in the U.S. Customs Service. Somehow there was just the mention of that name and the Spirit confirmed it. Because of time pressures he was called by telephone to preside over the mission.

I visited him a few weeks later. He was living in Washington, D.C. In his employment he was within reach of the number one office in his category. His lifetime had been spent progressing through the ranks, with the thought that perhaps one day he would stand at the head of that division. His senior officer had indicated that because of a health problem he himself would retire early, and that this man was being recommended for the position he was vacating. It was just at that time that the telephone call came.

I wanted to get acquainted with him, and he invited me to stay overnight. He brought me a message from his superior. The message was this: "Tell that Brother Packer of yours that you're no missionary; I've worked with you for thirty years, and you haven't converted me. Tell them they're making a mistake. And *you're* making a mistake. You're a fool." (I'm leaving out one word.) "If you will give up your retirement and all that you've reached for—why? Why would you do it?"

Simple answer: he had been called. We live to know, in this church, that the response to a call does not depend on the testimony and witness of the one who delivers the call. It depends, rather, on the testimony and witness of the one who receives it.

It was very interesting. We were looking for a man who spoke French. It was not until after he was in the mission field and we had some opportunities and responsibilities relating to problems of some members we had in Spain that we discovered he also wrote and spoke Spanish fluently. I suppose if we'd searched through the Church for a man who spoke French, spoke Spanish, and had had some diplomatic experience, particularly as it related to customs work, we would have gone afar in the world and not found him. Yet he was found through the "chance" memory of one of the Brethren who had met a man a few years before in Korea who spoke French.

51

A Circle of Sisters

Years ago Sister Packer and I were visiting in Czechoslovakia, then behind the Iron Curtain. It was not easy to obtain visas, and we used great care so as not to jeopardize the safety and well-being of our members who for generations had struggled to keep their faith alive under conditions of unspeakable oppression.

The most memorable meeting was held in an upper room. The blinds were drawn. Even at night, those attending came at different times, one from one direction and one from another, so as to not call attention to themselves.

There were in attendance twelve sisters. We sang the hymns of Zion from songbooks—words without music—printed more than fifty years before. The Spiritual Living lesson was reverently given from the pages of a handmade manual. The few pages of Church literature we could get to them were typed at night, twelve carbon copies at a time, so as to share a few precious pages as widely as possible among the members.

I told those sisters that they belonged to the largest and

by all measure the greatest women's organization on earth. I quoted the Prophet Joseph Smith when he and the Brethren organized the Relief Society: "I now turn the key in [behalf of all women]."

This society is organized "according to your natures. . . . You are now placed in a situation in which you can act according to those sympathies [within you]. . . .

"If you live up to [these] privileges, the angels cannot be restrained from being your associates. . . .

"If this Society listen[s] to the counsel of the Almighty, through the heads of the Church, they shall have power to command queens in their midst" (*History of the Church,* 4:607, 605).

The Spirit was there. The lovely sister who had conducted with gentility and reverence wept openly.

I told them that upon our return I was assigned to speak at a Relief Society conference; could I deliver a message from them? Several of them made notes; each expression, every one, was in the spirit of giving—not of asking for anything. I shall never forget what one sister wrote: "A small circle of sisters send their own hearts and thoughts to all the sisters and beg the Lord to help us go forward."

Those words, *circle of sisters,* inspired me. I could see them standing in a circle that reached beyond that room and circled the world. I caught the same vision the apostles and prophets before us have had. The Relief Society is more than a circle now; it is more like a fabric of lace spread across the continents.

52

JUST ONE NAME

When I was organizing a stake in Samoa, there appeared before us in the interviews those wonderful Samoan brethren. One of them, a branch president, stood there—white shirt and a tie, lava-lava tied around his waist, barefooted. I told him we were organizing a stake and seeking a stake president and asking his suggestions on men who could fill that position. He said: "Yes, I know. I've prayed about this." And he continued, "I've come to know, by the voice of the Spirit, that Bishop Iona will be our new stake president."

He was right. But I wasn't anxious to have him make the announcement, and so I pressed him for another name.

He said, "No, just one name."

And I said, "Suppose he were not available or not eligible? Won't you suggest another name?" He stood there for a few minutes, and then, looking me straight in the eye, he said, "Elder Packer, are you asking me to go against the witness of the Spirit?" This wonderful man was possessed of that Spirit, as all of us can be, each of us answering the calls that come.

I affirm that the principle of revelation is constantly operative in the Church. Every week as the Apostles go out across the world, we have those experiences. We don't talk about them much. They are like the other miracles; they are the signs that follow those who believe. Let us all be reverently grateful for the sustaining power of the Spirit.

There have been many visitations to the [Salt Lake Temple].
President Lorenzo Snow saw the Savior there.
Most of these sacred experiences remain unpublished.
(From "The Temple, the Priesthood," ENSIGN,
May 1993, p. 20)

53

TEACH THEM TO TESTIFY

As a mission president, after hearing 206 missionaries stand up and make an expression, I finally came to the realization that we had heard 205 talks and only one testimony. The responses went something like this: "I'm grateful to be a missionary. I'm glad to be on a mission. I have a great companion. I love my companion. I've had good companions all the time. We had a great experience last week. We were tracting [and so on], and so you see how grateful I am to be on a mission. I have a testimony of this gospel. In the name of Jesus Christ, amen."

These missionaries had talked *about* testimony, but they had talked *around* it and *through* it, *underneath* it and *over* it, but never *to* it. It was marvelous what happened when we were able to show them how one bears testimony.

There are two ways to spell *bear*. *Bear* means to carry. All of the missionaries were bearing testimonies—carrying them all over New England. Everywhere they went their testimony went with them. There's another spelling to that word (and I wonder if we don't use the wrong one). *Bare* means to expose or reveal or make known. So we may carry a testimony but not reveal it! Teach our young people to bear their testimonies instead of saying they have testimonies and then not saying what they are. Teach them to bear direct witness.

While a witness may come from hearing a testimony borne by another, I am convinced that *the* witness comes when the Spirit of the Lord falls upon a man or woman when he or she is bearing testimony personally. Teach them to bear testimony. If they don't have a testimony it may come when they start bearing it.

I have seen one or two brethren even in our program who are very hesitant about bearing testimony. They get so concerned about knowledge, and they say: "Well, I don't really *know* that! I don't know whether I can say it." Well, you never will know *until* you say it. It isn't that seeing is believing; it's that believing is seeing. Can't you see where it is hidden? The skeptic, the sophisticate, the experimenter, the insincere never take that step and bear a testimony, and the witness is therefore held from them. Teach our young people to bear testimony—to bear testimony that Jesus is the Christ, that Joseph Smith is a prophet of God, that the Book of Mormon is true, that we lived before we came here, that Christ died to redeem us, and that He is the Son of God. As they testify of those things the Holy Ghost will bear witness in their hearts and it will be compounded a thousandfold more powerfully than if they just listen to a witness borne by others.

Teach our youth to bear testimony—direct, specific witness. I'm not offended at the testimony of little children who stand up and say, "I know." Some people criticize that, but it is the kindergarten of all spiritual learning. Teach our youth to bear witness and testimony, for therein they conform to a principle that opens the door so that great confirmation can come. As keepers of the faith, teach them to bear witness, to bear testimony.

After hearing nearly 205 expressions, almost the last missionary to bear testimony was new, and he was the kind of a boy who could not ever keep his hair combed. When it came his turn to bear testimony, he stood up and said one sentence. Suddenly I realized that I had heard 205 talks, but his was a testimony. He said, "I know that the gospel is true, I know that Joseph Smith is a prophet of God, and I know that Jesus is the Christ." He sat down. I learned a great deal from his sentence.

The Lord said that "every man might speak in the name of
God the Lord, even the Savior of the world" (D&C 1:20).
So humble men and women, and even young people,
not professionally trained for the ministry, carry on the work
of the Lord—many of us with little more
than the spiritual conviction that it is true.
(From "The Only True Church," ENSIGN,
November 1985, p. 80)

54

P.O. Box B

After the move to the Salt Lake Valley, notwithstanding the Saints' poverty and their struggles to establish homes, missionaries were called and sustained at general conference—often to the surprise of those called. In the general conference of October 1869, George Q. Cannon read the names of 141 brethren, called from many of the settlements, to go on short missions to the eastern states. Sixteen of them were bishops.

One message threads its way through the letters from the Brethren to local leaders: "We need more missionaries! We need more missionaries!" And this is the call we make today: We need more missionaries! We need more missionaries!

I have a letter signed by President John Taylor, written on April 12, 1884. It has an interesting letterhead:

The President's Office

The Church of Jesus Christ of Latter-day Saints

P.O. Box B

Salt Lake City, Utah

"P.O. Box B" became the symbol of the mission call for

generations of Latter-day Saints. A letter from Box B was a call to the mission field. Those letters came unannounced: no interviews, no asking whether it was convenient—just a letter from Box B, a call to serve.

Here is a response addressed to Box B, datelined Beaver, Utah, August 30, 1879:

> President John Taylor
> Dear Brother,
>
> Yours of the 27 instance notifying myself to make my arrangements to go on a mission to the United States is to hand. You ask an answer of me. My answer is, I am glad that I am counted worthy by my brethren to go on a mission or fill any place of trust and I hope that I shall never do any thing to forfeit the confidence reposed.
> I know of nothing now to prevent my going as desired although plenty to do at home.

That simple phrase *although plenty to do at home* no doubt referred to a wife and family to feed and clothe, children to teach, a farm to keep, cows to milk, a garden to tend, a home to complete. All were set aside because a letter had come from Box B.

To continue the letter:

> I hold myself in readiness to act where I am supposed to do the most good. The work has to be done. The people warned. All should have a hand in the great work of the last days. I hope this may find you well in body and mind.
> Praying God to bless and preserve you to perform the grate labors that devolves upon you.
> Your brother in the gospel,
> J.R. Murdock

One Sunday afternoon after church, George T. Benson and his family stopped at the store in Whitney, Idaho, to pick up the mail. The store was closed, but the letter boxes were open. As they rode home in the buggy, Sister Benson sorted through the letters and found one from Box B. They sold part of the farm to finance Brother Benson on his mission. He left his wife and seven children (including young Ezra) and answered the call. The eighth child was born four months after he arrived in the mission field.

Young David Kennedy was engaged to lovely Lenora Bingham. They had sent out their wedding announcements. Then came a letter from Box B. He hurried to his bishop, who counseled them to marry—and then for him to leave immediately on his mission. She would wait and support him.

William W. Phelps wrote:

> *I go devoted to His cause,*
> *And to His will resigned;*
> *His presence will supply the loss*
> *Of all I leave behind.*
>
> *I go because the Master calls;*
> *He's made my duty plain—*
> *No danger can the heart appall*
> *When Jesus stoops to reign.*

Perhaps a few refused the call from Box B, but we have no record of them.

Much has changed since those Box B days, but one thing must not change. We must not—we cannot—lose the spirit of the call, for it is a demonstration of the power of revelation.

55

IS IT TRUE?

Now, someone may say, "Well, I've never heard that in general conference." I remember once that Brother Lee gave a talk at BYU, and he told me that he felt some unusual inspiration in that talk and gave emphasis to a point that he had not intended to discuss. A few days later one of the professors from BYU called at his office and said, "Brother Lee, I was very interested in your talk. I was very interested in one point particularly."

Brother Lee said, "Yes, I was quite interested too."

The professor said, "Would you mind citing the reference and the authority for that?"

Brother Lee thought for a few minutes and said, "Yes, the reference for that is Elder Harold B. Lee of the Council of the Twelve Apostles, speaking at a devotional assembly at BYU," and then he gave the date of his sermon.

The point I make, simply, is this: It isn't a question of who said it or when; the question is whether it is true.

56

THE LIGHT ON THE SHORE

In 1971 I was assigned to stake conferences in Western Samoa, including the organization of the Upolo West Stake. After the necessary interviews on Upolo Island, we chartered a plane to the Island of Savaii to hold a midweek stake conference of the Savaii Stake.

There were in our party besides myself and John H. Groberg, now of the First Quorum of Seventy and then a regional representative, President Wayne Shute of the Samoan Mission, now a professor of education at BYU, Mark Littleford, superintendent of Church Schools in Samoa, and Brother Laeausa, a Samoan "talking chief" who would represent us in some ceremonies.

The plane landed on a grass field at Faala and was to return the next afternoon to take us back to Apia on Upolo Island. The next afternoon it was raining a little. Knowing the plane would not land on the grassy field, we drove to the west end of Savaii where there was a runway of sorts atop a coral waterbreak. We waited until dark; no plane arrived. We were finally able to learn by radiophone that it was storming on Upolo Island and that the plane could not take off. We were able as well to tell them we would come by boat and to have someone meet us at Mulisanua.

We then drove about three hours back around the island to Saleleloga. There President Tuioti, a counselor in the Savaii Stake presidency, arranged for a boat and obtained the necessary police permit to make the night crossing.

As we pulled out of port, the captain of the forty-foot boat, the *Tori Tula*, asked President Shute if he happened to have a flashlight. Fortunately he did, and he made a present of it to the captain. We made the thirteen-mile crossing to Mulisanua on Upolo Island on very rough seas. None of us realized that a ferocious tropical storm had hit Upolo Island.

At Mulisanua there is one narrow passage through the reef. A light on the hill above the beach marked that narrow passage. There was a second lower light on the beach. When a boat was maneuvered so that the two lights were one above the other, it was lined up properly to pass through the reef.

But that night there was only one light. Someone was on the landing waiting to meet us, but the crossing had taken much longer than usual. After waiting for hours, watching for signs of our boat, they tired and fell asleep in the car, neglecting to turn on the lower light.

The captain maneuvered the boat toward the single light on shore while a crewman held a flashlight off the bow. It seemed like the boat would struggle up a mountainous wave and then pause in exhaustion at the crest of it with the propellers out of the water. The vibration of the propellers would shake the boat nearly to pieces before it slid down the other side.

We could hear the breakers crashing over the reef. When we were close enough to see them with the flashlight, the captain frantically shouted, "Reverse," and backed away to try again to locate the passage through the reef. After many attempts, he knew it would be impossible to find the opening. All we could do was try to reach the harbor in Apia, twenty miles away. We were helpless against the ferocious power of the elements. I do not remember ever being where it was so dark.

We were lying spread-eagled on the cover of the cargo hold, holding on with our hands on one side, with our toes locked on the other to keep from being washed overboard. Mark Littleford lost hold and was thrown against the low iron rail. His head was cut front and back, but the rail kept him from being washed away.

As we set out for Apia Harbor, I kept a post on the rail in line of sight with the one light on shore. We made no progress for the first hour even though the engine was full throttle. Eventually we moved ahead, and near daylight we pulled into Apia Harbor. Boats were lashed to boats several deep at the pier. We crawled across several of them, trying not to disturb those sleeping on deck. We made our way to Pesanga, dried our clothing, and headed for Vailuutai to organize the new stake.

I do not know who had been waiting for us at Mulisanua. I refused to let them tell me. Nor do I care now. But it is true that without that light, the lower light—the light that failed—we all might have been lost.

57

THE CERTAIN SOUND
OF THE TRUMPET

Years ago, as an Assistant to the Twelve, I accompanied Elder Spencer W. Kimball, then a member of the Twelve, to a conference of what was then known as the Southwest Indian Mission. We had two hundred missionaries assembled in the stake center on Main Street in the middle of the business district in Snowflake, Arizona.

In those days the missionaries lived in huts and makeshift quarters scattered across the reservations. I think I am not uncharitable if I describe their circumstances as being dismal and forbidding. It was difficult to give the missionaries some courage. They felt self-conscious and inadequate.

In the earlier days of the Church there was a strength that missionaries received from street meetings. In the Southwest Indian Mission there were very few communities, much less streets. The people were scattered and the missionaries needed some help and encouragement. Brother Kimball was determined to lift their morale, to rally them to service.

Brother Kimball was a musician. He had a very fine voice and could play the piano. He also understood young people. On that occasion we did something that I had never done before, nor have I done it since. I suppose it would not be appropriate except under those very circumstances.

What we did was this: After meeting for much of the day, we were invited to take our hymnbooks and stand and sing "Ye Elders of Israel." As we were singing, Brother Kimball gave the signal for us all to follow him. The side doors of the stake center were swung open, and we followed Brother Kimball down the walk and out into the middle of Main Street in Snowflake, Arizona. All traffic stopped.

The missionaries followed, falling into ranks of four, two hundred of them, singing "Ye Elders of Israel." Brother Kimball and I and President J. Elmer Baird, the mission president, were in the lead. Singing the stirring anthems from the hymnbook all the way, we marched down Main Street through the business district for four blocks, turned one block to the left, marched four blocks back, again around the corner and into the stake center, still singing.

That did something to that mission. The young elders who had never held a street meeting were imbued with courage they had not known before. I learned something from that experience. I learned that you can rally the young elders of Israel. I learned that they will march to a certain sound of the trumpet.

In my generation, we marched away to war. We did not wait to be conscripted. Tyler Nelson and Elmer Yates and Wilford Stokes and hundreds of thousands of others did not return. But that was the price that had to be paid for the cause, and we all went willingly. The youth of Zion will serve a cause and they won't have to be conscripted. They will go if they are taught and they are *called!*

There is a stirring song entitled "Called to Serve" that was once often heard in a Primary setting but is now in our regular hymnbook. Oh that it could be carried in the heart of every Latter-day Saint young man as he grows toward manhood! Oh that it could be sung, occasionally at least, in every zone in every mission in the world!

> *Called to serve him, heav'nly King of glory,*
> *Chosen e'er to witness for his name;*
> *Far and wide we tell the Father's story,*
> *Far and wide his love proclaim.*
>
> *Called to know the richness of his blessing—*
> *Sons and daughters, children of a King—*
> *Glad of heart, his holy name confessing,*
> *Praises unto him we bring.*
>
> *Onward, ever onward, as we glory in his name;*
> *Onward, ever onward, as we glory in his name;*
> *Forward, pressing forward, as a triumph song we sing.*
> *God our strength will be; press forward ever,*
> *Called to serve our King.*
>   (Hymns, no. 249)

58

WANTING TO DO HIS WILL

Practice grows into self-discipline, which is really the "only" kind of discipline. The discipline that comes from within is that which makes a young person decide that he wants to be free to play the piano and play it well. Therefore, he is willing to pay the price. Then he can be free from supervision, from pressure, from whatever forms of persuasion parents use.

In our family I have a key that I use, a kind of fatherly key. With my children I know when it is time to lift supervision. As I meet young people around the Church, they are always saying, "When will my parents ever think I have enough maturity to act for myself?" I know when with my family. I have employed this key. I know that they are ready for full freedom in any field of endeavor the very minute they *stop resenting supervision*. At that moment I can back off, let them go alone, and really just be there to respond if they come for help.

When I was president of the New England Mission, the Tabernacle Choir was to sing at the world's fair in Montreal. The choir had one day unscheduled and suggested a concert in New England. One of the industrial leaders there asked for the privilege of sponsoring the concert.

Brother Condie and Brother Stewart came to Boston to discuss this matter. We met at the Boston airport and then drove to Attleboro, Massachusetts. Along the way Mr. Yeager asked about the concert. He said, "I would like to have a reception for the choir members. I could have it either at my home or at my club." He wanted to invite his friends, who were, of course, the prominent people of New England— indeed, of the nation. He talked of this, and then he asked about serving alcoholic beverages.

In answering, Brother Stewart said, "Well, Mr. Yeager, since it is your home and you are the host, I suppose you could do just as you want to do."

"That isn't what I had in mind," this wonderful man said. "I don't want to do what I want to do. I want to do what you want me to do."

Somewhere in that spirit is the key to freedom. We should put ourselves in a position before our Father in Heaven and say, individually, "I do not want to do what I want to do. I want to do what Thou wouldst have me do." Suddenly, like any father, the Lord could say, "Well, there is one more of my children almost free from the need of constant supervision."

59

BE COMFORTABLE WITH ALL

I recall an experience from pilot training in World War II. Air cadets were posted to colleges for ground training. We were assigned to Washington State University at Pullman. Eight of us who had never met were assigned to the same room. The first evening we introduced ourselves.

The first to speak was from a wealthy family in the East. He described the private schools he had attended. He said that each summer their family had "gone on the Continent." I had no way of knowing that meant they had traveled to Europe.

The father of the next had been governor of Ohio and at that time was in the president's cabinet.

And so it went. I was younger than most, and it was my first time away from home. Each had attended college. I had not. In fact, there was nothing to distinguish me at all.

When finally I got the courage to speak, I said, "I come from a little town in Utah that you have never heard of. I come from a large family, eleven children. My father is a mechanic and runs a little garage."

I said that my great-grandfather had joined the Church and come west with the pioneers.

To my surprise and relief, I was accepted. My faith and my obscurity were not a penalty.

From then until now I have never felt uncomfortable among people of wealth or achievement, of high station or of low. Nor have I been ashamed of my heritage or of the Church or felt the need to apologize for any of its doctrines, even those I could not defend to the satisfaction of everyone who might ask.

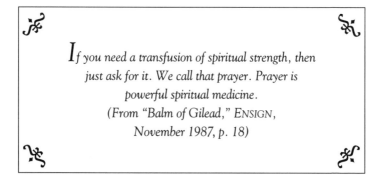

If you need a transfusion of spiritual strength, then just ask for it. We call that prayer. Prayer is powerful spiritual medicine.
(From "Balm of Gilead," ENSIGN,
November 1987, p. 18)

60

THE CHOICE—GOOD OR EVIL

Years ago I spent a day with Sister Packer in the record office in London. We were looking for Mary Haley. Like missionaries looking for living souls, we tracted through the pages of old record books. Some of them, I am sure, had not been opened for a hundred years.

I spent most of the day reading the minutes of the overseers of the workhouse—which was really the poorhouse.

One entry told of a woman who had been dismissed from the workhouse and sent to prison. She was refused permission to leave to check on a report that her child was being badly abused at the workhouse school. In great frustration she had "willfully broken a window." And so they sent her to prison.

Another entry reported an inspection of the school. The doctor complained that piles of manure along the edge of the school yard blocked the drainage. Water and sewage had backed up into the yard until the mire was ankle deep. Because of the cold and the poor condition of the children's shoes, many children were ill.

The record of dismissals listed "dead" or "died" time after

time, with an explanation: "complaint," "fever," "consump-
tion," "dropsy."

We found Mary Haley! She married Edward Sayers, and
they had eleven children. Six of them died before they were
seven years of age, one from burns. To our knowledge, only
one of the eleven grew to maturity.

That was Eleanor Sayers, my wife's great-grandmother.
She was born at Pullham, Norfolk, in the Depwade Union
Workhouse and was the first of her family to join the Church.
She died of cancer in a dismal London hospital.

The lives of those souls, our forebears, were characterized
from beginning to end by both poverty and obscurity.

Before Eleanor Sayers Harman died, she gave all of her
funds to her daughter Edith and counseled her to go to
America.

Edith had been cast out by her husband when she joined
the Church. She and eight-year-old Nellie left England with
the flimsy assurance that a missionary *thought* his family in
Idaho might take them in until they could be located.

Nellie was my wife's mother; Edith, her grandmother. I
knew them well. They were women of special nobility.

Our lineage runs also to the stately manor houses of
England, well connected with the courts of kings, where culture and plenty were much in evidence. But the dignity and
worth of those forebears is not more, and may well be less,
than that of Eleanor Sayers.

Eleanor, Edith and Nellie—all were women of a special
nobility, the royalty of righteousness. We want our children
to remember that their lineage runs to the poorhouse in
Pullham, Norfolk, and to remember this: It is the misappre-
hension of most people that if you are good, really good, at

what you do, you will eventually be both widely known and well compensated.

It is the understanding of almost everyone that success, to be complete, must include a generous portion of both fame and fortune as essential ingredients. The world seems to work on that premise. The premise is false. It is not true. The Lord taught otherwise.

True happiness is not based on wealth or fame. I want you, our children, to know this truth: You need not be either rich or hold high position to be completely successful and truly happy. In fact, if these things come to you, and they may, true success must be achieved in spite of them, not because of them.

It is remarkably difficult to teach this truth. If one who is not well known, and not well compensated, claims that he has learned for himself that neither fame nor fortune are essential to success, we tend to reject his statement as self-serving. What else could he say and not count himself a failure?

If someone who has possession of fame or fortune asserts that neither matters to success or happiness, we suspect that his expression can also be self-serving, even patronizing.

Therefore, we will not accept as reliable authorities either those who have fame and fortune or those who have not. We question that either can be an objective witness.

That leaves only one course open to us: trial and error—to learn for oneself, by experience, about prominence and wealth or their opposites.

We thereafter struggle through life, perhaps missing both fame and fortune, to finally learn one day that one can, indeed, succeed without possessing either. Or we may, one day, have both and learn that neither has made us happy;

neither is basic to the recipe for true success and for complete happiness. That is a very slow way to learn.

We come into mortal life to receive a body and to be tested, to learn to choose.

We want our children and their children to know that the choice of life is not between fame and obscurity, nor is the choice between wealth and poverty. The choice is between good and evil, and that is a very different matter indeed.

INDEX

ABOUT THE AUTHOR

Boyd K. Packer, Acting President of the Quorum of the Twelve Apostles, has been a member of the Quorum since 1970 and a General Authority since 1961. Immediately prior to that, he was supervisor of seminaries and institutes for the Church. He is a former president of the New England States Mission.

He was born in Brigham City, Utah. Following his graduation from high school, he served as a pilot in the U.S. Air Force during World War II. After the war he obtained his bachelor's and master's degrees, and then received his doctorate in education from Brigham Young University. He is the author of many books, including *The Things of the Soul, Teach Ye Diligently, The Holy Temple, "That All May Be Edified," Let Not Your Heart Be Troubled,* and *Memborable Stories and Parables by Boyd K. Packer.*

President Packer is married to Donna Edith Smith, and the couple have ten children.